The Celebration Journal

Debra Hewitt

Shadow River Books

Also by Debra Hewitt

Chasing Your Dream: A Guided Journal
Intentions and Reflections Weekly Planner
The Road to Success Day Planner

THE CELEBRATION JOURNAL
Copyright © 2017 by Debra Hewitt
All rights reserved

Individual results will vary.
This title is sold with no warranty as to your success.

Published in the United States by Shadow River Books

Paperback ISBN: 978-1-945472-08-4

www.shadowriverbooks.com

Welcome to *The Celebration Journal*

You have big goals. You know exactly where you want to be a year from now. But it's a long way off, and sometimes it feels like a really long slog. There are so many ways and places to get off track, get discouraged, give up.

Or maybe you're not at all sure where you're heading. You wish you had a way to see how your daily grind adds up to something, but you're really afraid it doesn't. Life seems like one chore after another, leaving you feeling unsuccessful and unmotivated.

In either case you can benefit from *The Celebration Journal*. You see, I'm convinced that you have small victories worth celebrating every day. You just have to learn to notice them.

What do I mean by small victories? The little bit of progress you might ignore because you are so focused on the finish line. The times you want to procrastinate but don't. The things that scare you but you steel yourself to do anyway. Recognizing these moments will help you maintain your enthusiasm during long projects and help you see what it is that makes each day meaningful.

Many productivity experts recommend quarterly rather than annual goal setting so I have designed *The Celebration Journal* for ninety days use. But you aren't tied to the calendar. The pages are undated so you can make entries every day or skip the weekends. Even take a week off for vacation. It's up to you. You can't fail at this.

Whatever your goal is, losing weight or writing a novel, this approach can help you enjoy the process. Try it for ninety days. Let me help you make every day a celebration.

For tips on setting and reaching your goals, visit:
www.shadowriverbooks.com

How to Use This Journal

Any number relevant to your goal:

My Goal — A reminder of your project: sign 4 new clients this month; finish the first draft of novel; or lose 10 pounds by June

 # days to deadline, pounds lost, money saved

My Affirmation for Today

Positive words that will help you turn wishes into action:
I am willing to work hard for my success or
I believe in my talent strongly enough to keep learning.

My Schedule

Keep track of appointments and meetings here.

Schedule work in blocks to avoid losing time by constantly switching from one activity to another.

Details

What you need to take to a meeting

Information you're waiting for

Prayer lists

Grocery lists

Addresses, phone numbers

Notes

Whatever you want or need to remember from today

Your reflections on the tip for the day

For more help setting goals and writing affirmations visit:
www.shadowriverbooks.com/celebration.html

The Celebration Journal

Fill in the circles completely or with stars.
1=not very, 2=somewhat, 3=very

How positive did I stay today?	★ ★ ○
How productive was I today?	★ ★ ★

Daily Tracker

habits/daily stats		Morning Pages	yes
		Water	||||
Devotions	yes	Walk	30 min

Relaxation
Try to include something fun in every day

Meals
... in case you're responsible for planning these or they are part of meeting your goals

Today I'm grateful
Fill this in anytime during the day. Try to think of something new for each entry.

My Tasks

- ○ List action items for today.
- ✗ Mark when completed.
- ○
- ○
- ○
- ○
- ○
- ○ Record items to be done in the future and move them later to the appropriate day.
- ○

Today I'm celebrating
No matter how your day went, find something to be pleased about and give yourself a moment to appreciate it. You might celebrate a milestone reached or simply keeping a positive attitude in the face of difficulties. This helps keep you motivated.

www.shadowriverbooks.com

Annual Plans and Reminders

Notes

January

February

March

April

May

June

July

August

September

October

November

December

The Celebration Journal

Quarterly ... Projects ... Deadlines ... Targets

Month

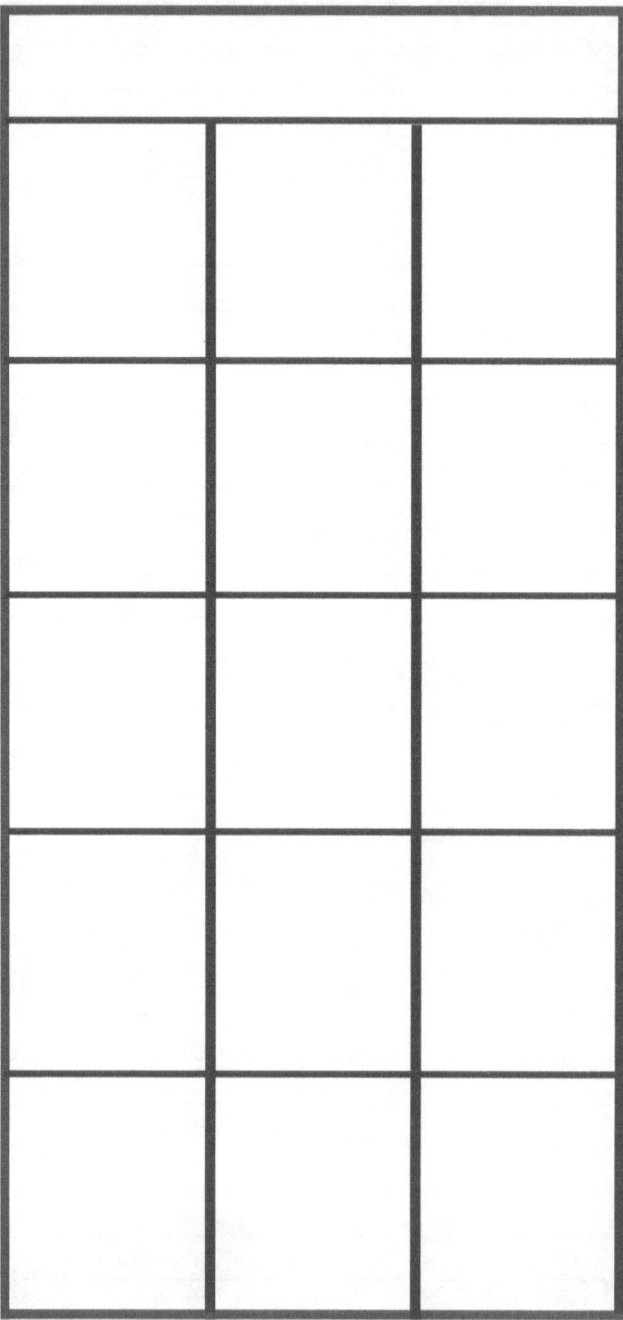

The Celebration Journal

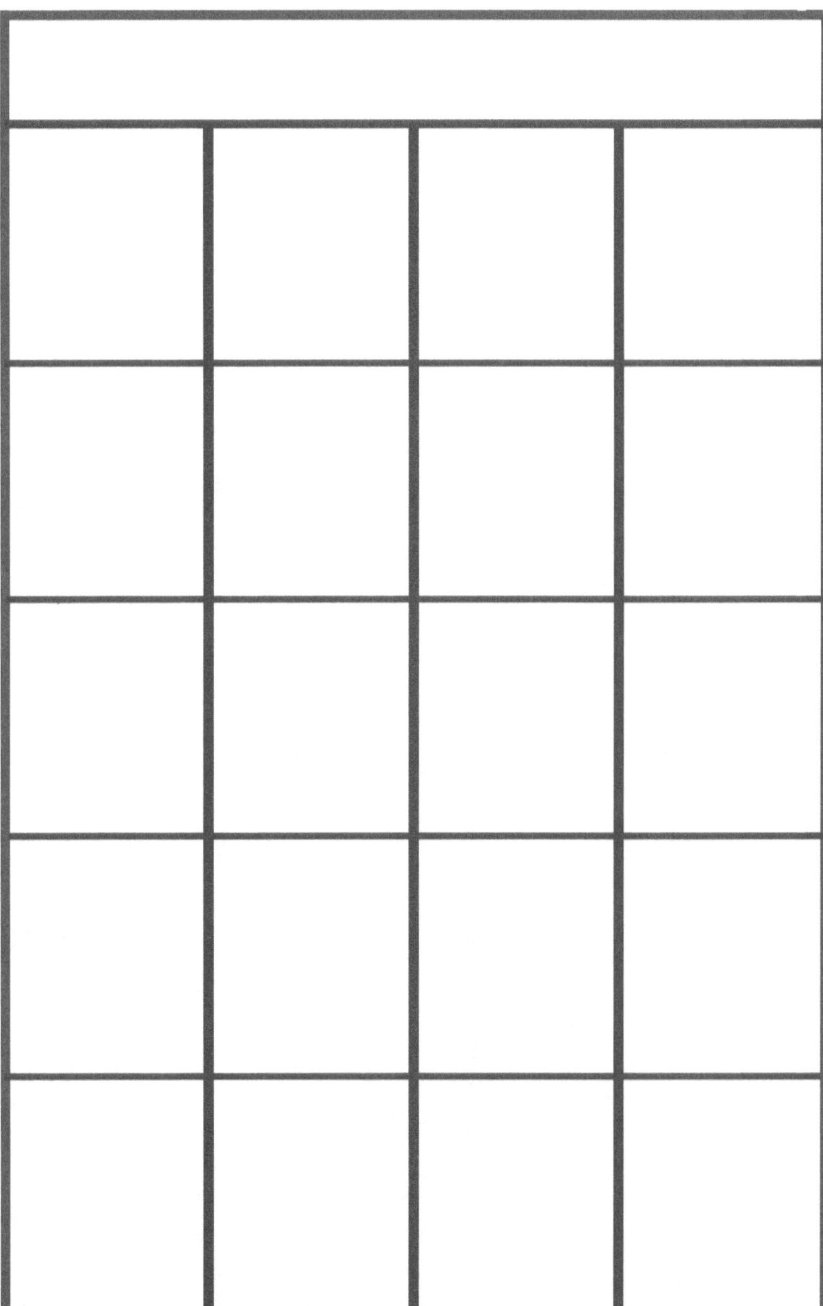

Month

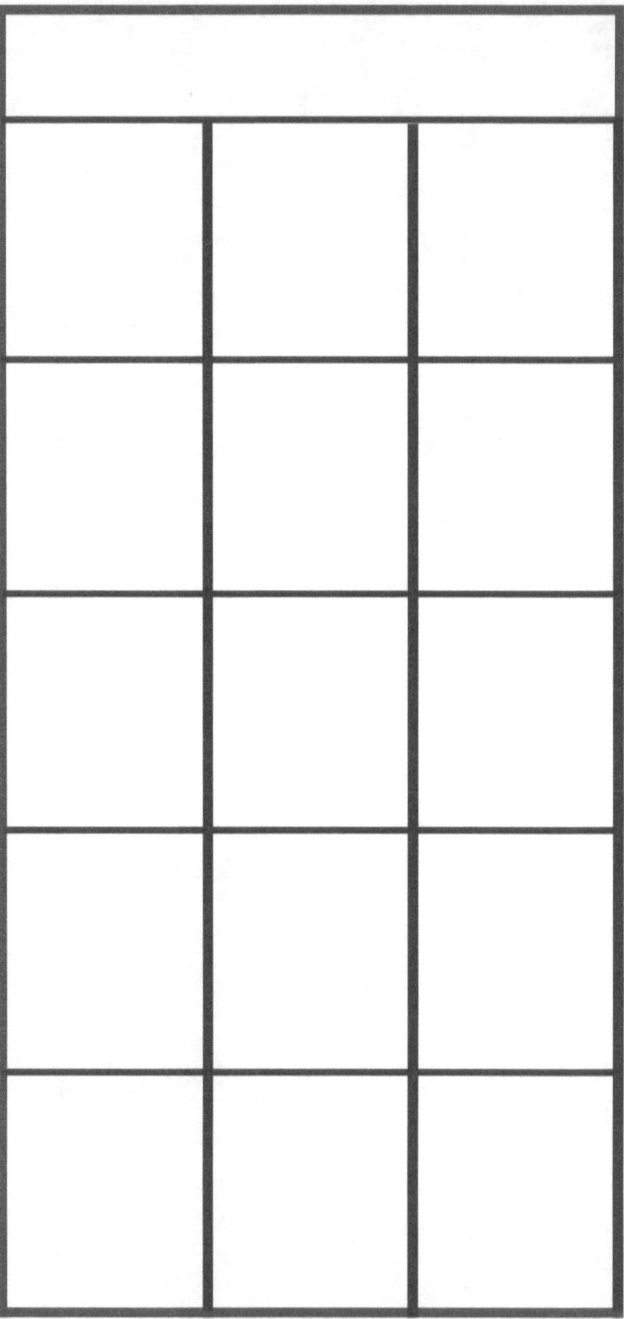

The Celebration Journal

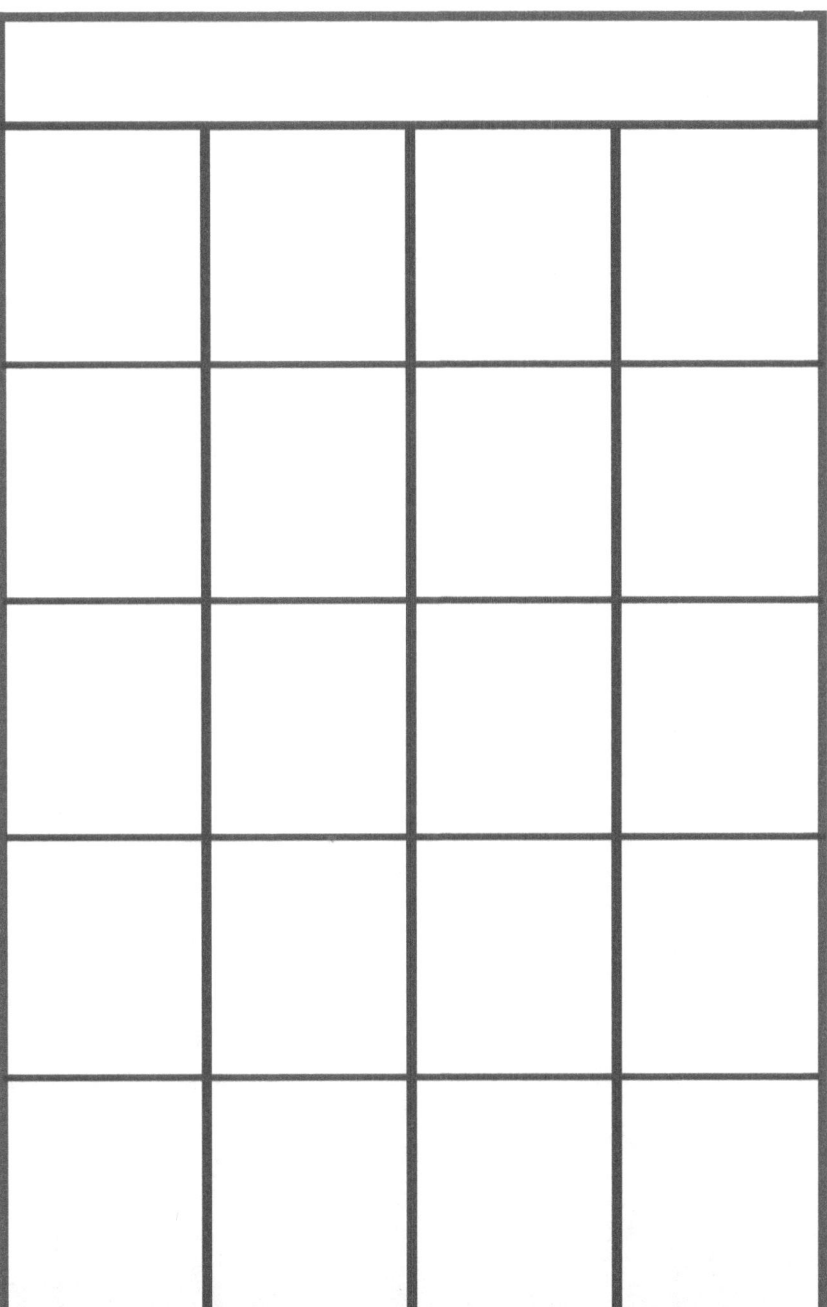

Month

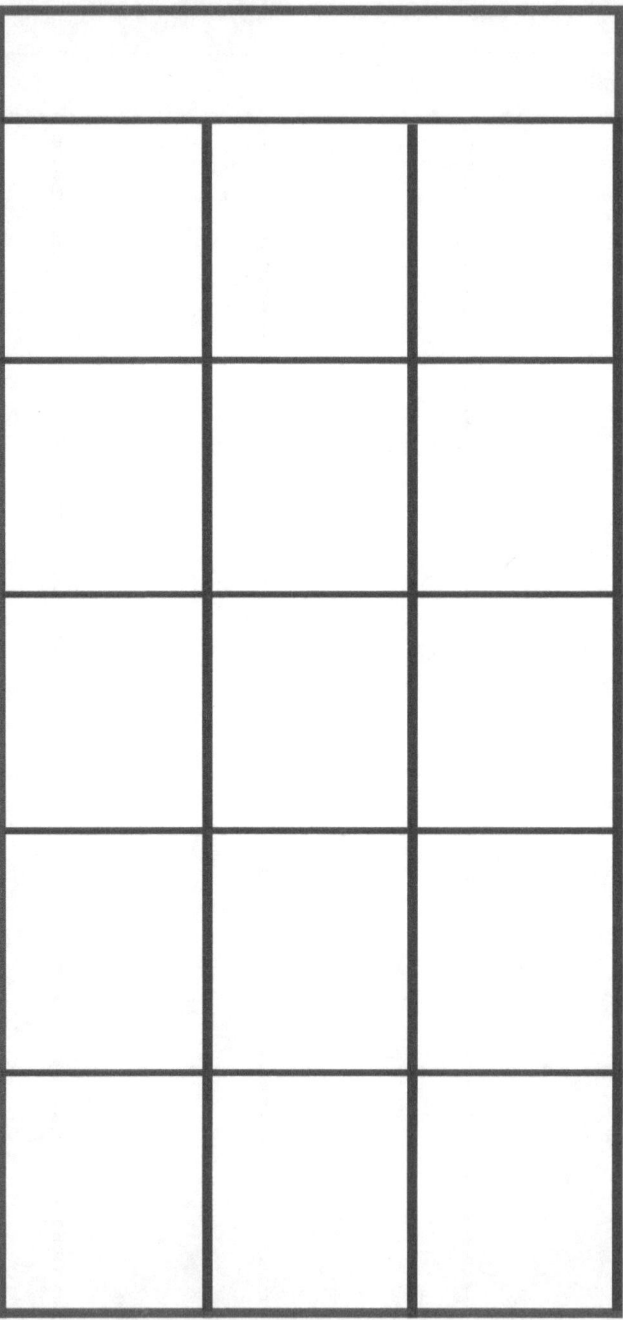

The Celebration Journal

date _____

Day 1 | My Goal

\#

My Affirmation for Today

My Schedule

Details

Notes

The Celebration Journal

Where do you want to go?
How will you know when you get there?

How positive did I stay today? ○○○
How productive was I today? ○○○

Daily Tracker

Relaxation

Meals

Today I'm grateful

My Tasks

Today I'm celebrating

www.shadowriverbooks.com

date _____

Day 2

My Goal

#

My Affirmation for Today

My Schedule

Details

Notes

The Celebration Journal

Set goals and actions that are worthy of the person you wish to become.

How positive did I stay today?
How productive was I today?

Relaxation

Daily Tracker

Meals

Today I'm grateful

My Tasks

-
-
-
-
-
-
-
-
-
-

Today I'm celebrating

date _____

Day 3 — My Goal   #

My Affirmation for Today

My Schedule   Details

Notes

The Celebration Journal

Thinking small is part of dreaming big.
What little thing today will help you reach your goal?

How positive did I stay today? ○ ○ ○
How productive was I today? ○ ○ ○

Daily Tracker

Relaxation

Meals

Today I'm grateful

My Tasks
- ○
- ○
- ○
- ○
- ○
- ○
- ○
- ○
- ○
- ○

Today I'm celebrating

www.shadowriverbooks.com

date _____

Day 4

My Goal

\#

My Affirmation for Today

My Schedule

Details

Notes

The Celebration Journal

Beginnings are usually difficult and time-consuming. Make allowances for that.

How positive did I stay today? ◯◯◯
How productive was I today? ◯◯◯

Relaxation

Daily Tracker

_____ ▢   _____ ▢
_____ ▢   _____ ▢
_____ ▢   _____ ▢

Meals

Today I'm grateful

My Tasks

◯
◯
◯
◯
◯
◯
◯
◯
◯
◯

Today I'm celebrating

www.shadowriverbooks.com

date _____

Day 5

My Goal

#

My Affirmation for Today

My Schedule

Details

Notes

The Celebration Journal

If gold stars work for you, then by all means,
give yourself a gold star. Why not?

How positive did I stay today?

How productive was I today?

Daily Tracker

Relaxation

Meals

Today I'm grateful

My Tasks

Today I'm celebrating

www.shadowriverbooks.com

date _____

Day 6

My Goal

#

My Affirmation for Today

My Schedule

Details

Notes

The Celebration Journal

When the task feels huge, try sneaking up on it.
Just commit to starting, nothing more.

How positive did I stay today?

How productive was I today?

Relaxation

Daily Tracker

Meals

Today I'm grateful

My Tasks

Today I'm celebrating

www.shadowriverbooks.com

date _____

Day 7

My Goal

#

My Affirmation for Today

My Schedule

Details

Notes

The Celebration Journal

The key to not getting discouraged with long projects is to focus on smaller goals along the way.

How positive did I stay today? ○○○
How productive was I today? ○○○

Relaxation

Daily Tracker

Meals

Today I'm grateful

My Tasks

Today I'm celebrating

www.shadowriverbooks.com

date _____

Day 8 | My Goal

#

My Affirmation for Today

My Schedule

Details

Notes

The Celebration Journal

Getting ready smooths the way to
actually doing what you want to do.

How positive did I stay today? ⚪⚪⚪
How productive was I today? ⚪⚪⚪

Relaxation

Daily Tracker

Meals

Today I'm grateful

My Tasks

Today I'm celebrating

www.shadowriverbooks.com

date _____

Day 9

My Goal

#

My Affirmation for Today

My Schedule

Details

Notes

The Celebration Journal

When doubts creep in, you must acknowledge and address them. What are you afraid of?

How positive did I stay today?
How productive was I today?

Daily Tracker

Relaxation

Meals

Today I'm grateful

My Tasks

Today I'm celebrating

www.shadowriverbooks.com

date _____

Day 10 | **My Goal** | #

My Affirmation for Today

My Schedule | **Details**

Notes

The Celebration Journal

Feeling overwhelmed? You may be overbooked.
How much are you trying to squeeze into your day?

How positive did I stay today? ○○○
How productive was I today? ○○○

Relaxation

Daily Tracker

_____ ☐   _____ ☐

_____ ☐   _____ ☐

_____ ☐   _____ ☐

Meals

Today I'm grateful

My Tasks

○
○
○
○
○
○
○
○
○

Today I'm celebrating

www.shadowriverbooks.com

date _____

Day 11

My Goal

#

My Affirmation for Today

My Schedule

Details

Notes

The Celebration Journal

If the goal matters, every inch closer is a win.

How positive did I stay today? ○○○
How productive was I today? ○○○

Relaxation

Daily Tracker

_____ ☐ _____ ☐
_____ ☐ _____ ☐
_____ ☐ _____ ☐

Meals

Today I'm grateful

My Tasks

○
○
○
○
○
○
○
○
○
○

Today I'm celebrating

date _____

Day 12

My Goal

#

My Affirmation for Today

My Schedule

Details

Notes

The Celebration Journal

It isn't always productive to adopt someone else's methods. Find the system that works for you.

How positive did I stay today?

How productive was I today?

Daily Tracker

Relaxation

Meals

Today I'm grateful

My Tasks

Today I'm celebrating

www.shadowriverbooks.com

date _____

Day 13

My Goal

#

My Affirmation for Today

My Schedule

Details

Notes

The Celebration Journal

If you find deadlines motivating, create several checkpoints along your path.

How positive did I stay today?
How productive was I today?

Relaxation

Daily Tracker

Meals

Today I'm grateful

My Tasks

Today I'm celebrating

www.shadowriverbooks.com

date _____

Day 14 | My Goal

\#

My Affirmation for Today

My Schedule

Details

Notes

The Celebration Journal

Know yourself. Don't set arbitrary deadlines if they foster a feeling of failure.

How positive did I stay today? ○○○
How productive was I today? ○○○

Daily Tracker

Relaxation

Meals

Today I'm grateful

My Tasks

Today I'm celebrating

www.shadowriverbooks.com

date _____

My Greatest Struggles So Far

My Schedule

Details

Notes

The Celebration Journal

You've done something today even if it wasn't what you planned. Can you celebrate that?

How positive did I stay today? ○○○
How productive was I today? ○○○

Relaxation

Daily Tracker

_____ ☐   _____ ☐
_____ ☐   _____ ☐
_____ ☐   _____ ☐

Meals

Today I'm grateful

My Tasks

○
○
○
○
○
○
○
○
○
○

Today I'm celebrating

www.shadowriverbooks.com

date _____

Day 16

My Goal

#

My Affirmation for Today

My Schedule

Details

Notes

The Celebration Journal

The timing may be wrong for you to take on a large project. If so, hit pause. We'll wait.

How positive did I stay today? ⚪⚪⚪
How productive was I today? ⚪⚪⚪

Daily Tracker

Relaxation

Meals

Today I'm grateful

My Tasks

☐
☐
☐
☐
☐
☐
☐
☐
☐

Today I'm celebrating

date _____

Day 17 My Goal

#

My Affirmation for Today

My Schedule

Details

Notes

The Celebration Journal

Doing what you feel born to do leads to your greatest happiness and long-term success.

How positive did I stay today? ⬜⬜⬜
How productive was I today? ⬜⬜⬜

Daily Tracker

_____ ☐   _____ ☐

_____ ☐   _____ ☐

_____ ☐   _____ ☐

Relaxation

Meals

Today I'm grateful

My Tasks

○
○
○
○
○
○
○
○
○
○

Today I'm celebrating

www.shadowriverbooks.com

date _____

Day 18   My Goal   #

My Affirmation for Today

My Schedule   Details

Notes

The Celebration Journal

Strive to improve, but avoid negative self-talk.
It isn't coddling to treat yourself with respect.

How positive did I stay today? ○○○
How productive was I today? ○○○

Daily Tracker

Relaxation

Meals

Today I'm grateful

My Tasks

- ○
- ○
- ○
- ○
- ○
- ○
- ○
- ○
- ○

Today I'm celebrating

www.shadowriverbooks.com

date _____

Day 19

My Goal

#

My Affirmation for Today

My Schedule

Details

Notes

The Celebration Journal

Never multitask. Even a little bit damages your ability to focus deeply at other times.

How positive did I stay today? ○○○
How productive was I today? ○○○

Daily Tracker

_____ ☐   _____ ☐
_____ ☐   _____ ☐
          ☐   _____ ☐

Today I'm grateful

Relaxation

Meals

My Tasks

- ○
- ○
- ○
- ○
- ○
- ○
- ○
- ○
- ○

Today I'm celebrating

www.shadowriverbooks.com

date _____

Day 20

My Goal

\#

My Affirmation for Today

My Schedule

Details

Notes

The Celebration Journal

Avoid burnout by making time for relaxation.
There's more to life than your achievements.

How positive did I stay today? ○○○
How productive was I today? ○○○

Daily Tracker

Relaxation

Meals

Today I'm grateful

My Tasks

○
○
○
○
○
○
○
○
○

Today I'm celebrating

www.shadowriverbooks.com

date _____

Day 21

My Goal

#

My Affirmation for Today

My Schedule

Details

Notes

The Celebration Journal

It's not a failure to adjust your expectations.
Adapting your plans shows a healthy grasp on reality.

How positive did I stay today? ○○○

How productive was I today? ○○○

Relaxation

Daily Tracker

Meals

Today I'm grateful

My Tasks

☐
☐
☐
☐
☐
☐
☐
☐
☐

Today I'm celebrating

www.shadowriverbooks.com

date _____

Day 22

My Goal

#

My Affirmation for Today

My Schedule

Details

Notes

The Celebration Journal

If possible, reserve your most productive time of day for your most demanding work.

How positive did I stay today?
How productive was I today?

Daily Tracker

Relaxation

Meals

Today I'm grateful

My Tasks

Today I'm celebrating

www.shadowriverbooks.com

date _____

Day 23 | My Goal | #

My Affirmation for Today

My Schedule | Details

Notes

The Celebration Journal

Instead of labeling yourself lazy or depressed, ask, "What's the problem? How can I fix it?"

How positive did I stay today?
How productive was I today?

Relaxation

Daily Tracker

Meals

Today I'm grateful

My Tasks

Today I'm celebrating

www.shadowriverbooks.com

date _____

Day 24

My Goal

#

My Affirmation for Today

My Schedule

Details

Notes

The Celebration Journal

What acts of courage do you need to celebrate?
How have you stepped out of your comfort zone?

How positive did I stay today?

How productive was I today?

Daily Tracker

Relaxation

Meals

Today I'm grateful

My Tasks

Today I'm celebrating

www.shadowriverbooks.com

date _____

Day 25

My Goal

#

My Affirmation for Today

My Schedule

Details

Notes

The Celebration Journal

Keep expecting to win even if you haven't yet.

How positive did I stay today? ⬜⬜⬜
How productive was I today? ⬜⬜⬜

Daily Tracker

Relaxation

Meals

Today I'm grateful

My Tasks

Today I'm celebrating

date _____

Day 26

My Goal

#

My Affirmation for Today

My Schedule

Details

Notes

The Celebration Journal

Waiting for an eventual payoff can be discouraging.
Stay motivated with small wins along the way.

How positive did I stay today? ○○○
How productive was I today? ○○○

Relaxation

Daily Tracker

Meals

Today I'm grateful

My Tasks

○
○
○
○
○
○
○
○
○

Today I'm celebrating

www.shadowriverbooks.com

date _____

Day 27 | My Goal

#

My Affirmation for Today

My Schedule

Details

Notes

The Celebration Journal

Would you want your child to give up on a dream because of fear? Why would you?

How positive did I stay today? ○ ○ ○
How productive was I today? ○ ○ ○

Daily Tracker

_____ ☐   _____ ☐
_____ ☐   _____ ☐
_____ ☐   _____ ☐

Today I'm grateful

Relaxation

Meals

My Tasks
- ○
- ○
- ○
- ○
- ○
- ○
- ○
- ○
- ○

Today I'm celebrating

www.shadowriverbooks.com

date _____

Day 28 | My Goal

\#

My Affirmation for Today

My Schedule

Details

Notes

The Celebration Journal

When you're new at something, you need to cut yourself some slack.

How positive did I stay today?
How productive was I today?

Relaxation

Daily Tracker

Meals

Today I'm grateful

My Tasks

Today I'm celebrating

www.shadowriverbooks.com

date _____

Day 29 My Goal #

My Affirmation for Today

My Schedule

Details

Notes

The Celebration Journal

How will you know when you reach your goal?
Is it measurable and specific?

How positive did I stay today?

How productive was I today?

Daily Tracker

Relaxation

Meals

Today I'm grateful

My Tasks

Today I'm celebrating

www.shadowriverbooks.com

date _____

Some Lessons Learned

My Schedule

Details

Notes

The Celebration Journal

Doggedly sticking to a plan that isn't working may be just another way to postpone success.

How positive did I stay today? ○○○
How productive was I today? ○○○

Daily Tracker

Relaxation

Meals

Today I'm grateful

My Tasks

Today I'm celebrating

www.shadowriverbooks.com

date _____

Day 31 | My Goal

\#

My Affirmation for Today

My Schedule

Details

Notes

The Celebration Journal

One of the best ways to combat resistance is to take a baby step in the direction you want to travel.

How positive did I stay today? ◉◉◉
How productive was I today? ◉◉◉

Daily Tracker

Relaxation

Meals

Today I'm grateful

My Tasks

Today I'm celebrating

date _____

Day 32   My Goal

\#

My Affirmation for Today

My Schedule

Details

Notes

The Celebration Journal

Most things worth doing take work.
Don't change course just because it isn't easy.

How positive did I stay today?
How productive was I today?

Relaxation

Daily Tracker

Meals

Today I'm grateful

My Tasks

Today I'm celebrating

www.shadowriverbooks.com

date _____

Day 33   My Goal   #

My Affirmation for Today

My Schedule   Details

Notes

The Celebration Journal

Keep your daily work bite-sized, and let the big picture inspire you not intimidate you.

How positive did I stay today? ● ● ●
How productive was I today? ● ● ●

Daily Tracker

Relaxation

Meals

Today I'm grateful

My Tasks

○
○
○
○
○
○
○
○
○
○

Today I'm celebrating

www.shadowriverbooks.com

date _____

Day 34 — My Goal

#

My Affirmation for Today

My Schedule

Details

Notes

The Celebration Journal

Your next step may be your breakthrough.
You wouldn't want to quit if you're almost finished.

How positive did I stay today?
How productive was I today?

Daily Tracker

Relaxation

Meals

Today I'm grateful

My Tasks

Today I'm celebrating

www.shadowriverbooks.com

date _____

| Day 35 | My Goal | # |

My Affirmation for Today

My Schedule

Details

Notes

The Celebration Journal

What excites you about your current project?
Start there when your enthusiasm lags.

How positive did I stay today?
How productive was I today?

Daily Tracker

Relaxation

Meals

Today I'm grateful

My Tasks

Today I'm celebrating

date _____

Day 36

My Goal

#

My Affirmation for Today

My Schedule

Details

Notes

The Celebration Journal

Be aware that periods of high stress are poor times for new projects or major decisions.

How positive did I stay today? ◯◯◯
How productive was I today? ◯◯◯

Daily Tracker

Relaxation

Meals

Today I'm grateful

My Tasks

- ◯
- ◯
- ◯
- ◯
- ◯
- ◯
- ◯
- ◯
- ◯

Today I'm celebrating

www.shadowriverbooks.com

date _____

Day 37 | My Goal

#

My Affirmation for Today

My Schedule

Details

Notes

The Celebration Journal

Don't berate yourself for missing
self-imposed deadlines. Renegotiate.

How positive did I stay today?
How productive was I today?

Daily Tracker

Relaxation

Meals

Today I'm grateful

My Tasks

- ○
- ○
- ○
- ○
- ○
- ○
- ○
- ○
- ○

Today I'm celebrating

date _____

Day 38 My Goal   #

My Affirmation for Today

My Schedule   Details

Notes

The Celebration Journal

One step closer is one step closer.
Don't disparage modest progress.

How positive did I stay today? ○○○
How productive was I today? ○○○

Daily Tracker

Relaxation

Meals

Today I'm grateful

My Tasks

- ○
- ○
- ○
- ○
- ○
- ○
- ○
- ○
- ○

Today I'm celebrating

www.shadowriverbooks.com

date _____

Day 39 | My Goal

\#

My Affirmation for Today

My Schedule

Details

Notes

The Celebration Journal

Don't give up. Find your own rhythm and carry on.

How positive did I stay today? ☐☐☐
How productive was I today? ☐☐☐

Daily Tracker

_____ ☐   _____ ☐
_____ ☐   _____ ☐
_____ ☐   _____ ☐

Today I'm grateful

Relaxation

Meals

My Tasks

○
○
○
○
○
○
○
○
○
○

Today I'm celebrating

Day 40 | date _____

My Goal

#

My Affirmation for Today

My Schedule

Details

Notes

The Celebration Journal

When we've tried and failed,
we can still celebrate trying.

How positive did I stay today? ◯◯◯
How productive was I today? ◯◯◯

Daily Tracker

____ ☐   ____ ☐

____ ☐   ____ ☐

____ ☐   ____ ☐

Today I'm grateful

Relaxation

Meals

My Tasks

◯
◯
◯
◯
◯
◯
◯
◯
◯

Today I'm celebrating

date _____

Day 41 My Goal   #

My Affirmation for Today

My Schedule   Details

Notes

The Celebration Journal

Judge your results not in terms of how far you have to go but how far you've already come.

How positive did I stay today? ○○○

How productive was I today? ○○○

Relaxation

Daily Tracker

_____ ☐   _____ ☐

_____ ☐   _____ ☐

_____ ☐   _____ ☐

Meals

Today I'm grateful

My Tasks

○
○
○
○
○
○
○
○
○
○

Today I'm celebrating

www.shadowriverbooks.com

date _____

Day 42

My Goal

#

My Affirmation for Today

My Schedule

Details

Notes

The Celebration Journal

Try to tune in to your growth
as well as your successes.

How positive did I stay today? ○ ○ ○
How productive was I today? ○ ○ ○

Daily Tracker

Relaxation

Meals

Today I'm grateful

My Tasks
○
○
○
○
○
○
○
○
○
○

Today I'm celebrating

www.shadowriverbooks.com

date _____

Day 43

My Goal

#

My Affirmation for Today

My Schedule

Details

Notes

The Celebration Journal

Keep going, keep going, keep going.
You're blazing a trail for those who follow.

How positive did I stay today? ◯◯◯
How productive was I today? ◯◯◯

Daily Tracker

Relaxation

Meals

Today I'm grateful

My Tasks

Today I'm celebrating

date _____

Day 44

My Goal

#

My Affirmation for Today

My Schedule

Details

Notes

The Celebration Journal

Most successful people had to cope with many failures on the way to their goals.

How positive did I stay today?

How productive was I today?

Daily Tracker

Relaxation

Meals

Today I'm grateful

My Tasks

Today I'm celebrating

date _____

Day 45

Past Successes Which Encourage Me

My Schedule

Details

Notes

The Celebration Journal

We sometimes forget how far we've come.
What progress have you made in the past year?

How positive did I stay today?
How productive was I today?

Daily Tracker

Relaxation

Meals

Today I'm grateful

My Tasks

Today I'm celebrating

date _____

Day 46

My Goal

\#

My Affirmation for Today

My Schedule

Details

Notes

The Celebration Journal

If it's time to step up the pace, frame it as a win,
a challenge you are now ready to tackle.

How positive did I stay today? ◯ ◯ ◯

How productive was I today? ◯ ◯ ◯

Daily Tracker

Relaxation

Meals

Today I'm grateful

My Tasks

Today I'm celebrating

www.shadowriverbooks.com

date _____

Day 47 My Goal

#

My Affirmation for Today

My Schedule

Details

Notes

The Celebration Journal

The journey may be long, but every day can be a celebration.

How positive did I stay today? ☐☐☐
How productive was I today? ☐☐☐

Daily Tracker

Relaxation

Meals

Today I'm grateful

My Tasks
○
○
○
○
○
○
○
○
○

Today I'm celebrating

www.shadowriverbooks.com

Day 48

date _____

My Goal

#

My Affirmation for Today

My Schedule

Details

Notes

The Celebration Journal

If you have survived a setback or lost with good grace, that is something to celebrate.

How positive did I stay today?
How productive was I today?

Daily Tracker

Relaxation

Meals

Today I'm grateful

My Tasks

Today I'm celebrating

date _____

Day 49 | My Goal | #

My Affirmation for Today

My Schedule | Details

Notes

The Celebration Journal

Do you believe in what you are doing?
Do you believe enough to give it your all?

How positive did I stay today? ⬜⬜⬜
How productive was I today? ⬜⬜⬜

Daily Tracker

Relaxation

Meals

Today I'm grateful

My Tasks

- ○
- ○
- ○
- ○
- ○
- ○
- ○
- ○
- ○

Today I'm celebrating

www.shadowriverbooks.com

date _____

Day 50 My Goal   #

My Affirmation for Today

My Schedule   Details

Notes

The Celebration Journal

Use your affirmations to resolve to work hard and believe in yourself. Focus on choices and actions.

How positive did I stay today?
How productive was I today?

Daily Tracker

Relaxation

Meals

Today I'm grateful

My Tasks

- ○
- ○
- ○
- ○
- ○
- ○
- ○
- ○
- ○

Today I'm celebrating

date _____

Day 51

My Goal

#

My Affirmation for Today

My Schedule

Details

Notes

The Celebration Journal

If you're feeling reluctant, ask what your subconscious is trying to protect you from.

How positive did I stay today? ○○○
How productive was I today? ○○○

Daily Tracker

Relaxation

Meals

Today I'm grateful

My Tasks

Today I'm celebrating

www.shadowriverbooks.com

date _____

Day 52 | My Goal

#

My Affirmation for Today

My Schedule

Details

Notes

The Celebration Journal

Sometimes what feels like laziness is really fear.
Maybe you need a lifeline more than a whip.

How positive did I stay today?
How productive was I today?

Daily Tracker

Relaxation

Meals

Today I'm grateful

My Tasks

Today I'm celebrating

www.shadowriverbooks.com

date _____

Day 53

My Goal

#

My Affirmation for Today

My Schedule

Details

Notes

The Celebration Journal

How would a loving friend encourage you today? Be that friend for yourself.

How positive did I stay today? ⚪⚪⚪
How productive was I today? ⚪⚪⚪

Daily Tracker

Relaxation

Meals

Today I'm grateful

My Tasks

Today I'm celebrating

www.shadowriverbooks.com

date _____

Day 54

My Goal

#

My Affirmation for Today

My Schedule

Details

Notes

The Celebration Journal

If you're feeling proud, take a picture. You'll need to remember the moment. Then get back to work.

How positive did I stay today?
How productive was I today?

Daily Tracker

Relaxation

Meals

Today I'm grateful

My Tasks

- ○
- ○
- ○
- ○
- ○
- ○
- ○
- ○
- ○
- ○

Today I'm celebrating

www.shadowriverbooks.com

date _____

Day 55

My Goal

\#

My Affirmation for Today

My Schedule

Details

Notes

The Celebration Journal

No matter how many failures you have,
they just mean you haven't succeeded . . . yet.

How positive did I stay today?
How productive was I today?

Daily Tracker

Relaxation

Meals

Today I'm grateful

My Tasks

Today I'm celebrating

date _____

Day 56 My Goal

\#

My Affirmation for Today

My Schedule

Details

Notes

The Celebration Journal

If it's hard to muster enthusiasm, maybe your goal matters more to others than it does to you.

How positive did I stay today? ○○○
How productive was I today? ○○○

Daily Tracker

Relaxation

Meals

Today I'm grateful

My Tasks

Today I'm celebrating

www.shadowriverbooks.com

date _____

Day 57   My Goal   #

My Affirmation for Today

My Schedule   Details

Notes

The Celebration Journal

When you're afraid to take an action,
there may be a good reason. Try to understand it.

How positive did I stay today?

How productive was I today?

Daily Tracker

Relaxation

Meals

Today I'm grateful

My Tasks

Today I'm celebrating

date _____

Day 58

My Goal

#

My Affirmation for Today

My Schedule

Details

Notes

The Celebration Journal

If you're experiencing burnout,
set aside time for activities that renew you.

How positive did I stay today?
How productive was I today?

Daily Tracker

Relaxation

Meals

Today I'm grateful

My Tasks

Today I'm celebrating

www.shadowriverbooks.com

date _____

Day 59   My Goal   #

My Affirmation for Today

My Schedule   Details

Notes

If you can't see the finish line, you don't know how close you may be to success. You mustn't lose heart.

How positive did I stay today?
How productive was I today?

Daily Tracker

Relaxation

Meals

Today I'm grateful

My Tasks

Today I'm celebrating

date _____

Past Failures That Still Haunt Me

My Schedule

Details

Notes

The Celebration Journal

Fear defeats many of us because we credit one failure with the power to bar us and to brand us.

How positive did I stay today? ●●○ ●●○

How productive was I today? ●●○ ●●○

Daily Tracker

Relaxation

Meals

Today I'm grateful

My Tasks

Today I'm celebrating

date _____

Day 61

My Goal

#

My Affirmation for Today

My Schedule

Details

Notes

The Celebration Journal

If looking too far ahead is scary, focus on the next right move to make. Ease forward.

How positive did I stay today? ○○○
How productive was I today? ○○○

Daily Tracker

_____ ☐   _____ ☐
_____ ☐   _____ ☐
_____ ☐   _____ ☐

Relaxation

Meals

Today I'm grateful

My Tasks

○
○
○
○
○
○
○
○
○

Today I'm celebrating

www.shadowriverbooks.com

date _____

Day 62 My Goal   #

My Affirmation for Today

My Schedule   Details

Notes

The Celebration Journal

When your confidence lags, remind yourself of past successes. You can succeed again.

How positive did I stay today?

How productive was I today?

Daily Tracker

Relaxation

Meals

Today I'm grateful

My Tasks

Today I'm celebrating

date _____

Day 63

My Goal

#

My Affirmation for Today

My Schedule

Details

Notes

The Celebration Journal

Breaking a large project into smaller steps prevents panic and yields more wins along the way.

How positive did I stay today? ○○○
How productive was I today? ○○○

Daily Tracker

Relaxation

Meals

Today I'm grateful

My Tasks

Today I'm celebrating

date _____

Day 64

My Goal

\#

My Affirmation for Today

My Schedule

Details

Notes

The Celebration Journal

Nobody is ever an overnight success.
We just don't get the backstory while it's happening.

How positive did I stay today?
How productive was I today?

Daily Tracker

Relaxation

Meals

Today I'm grateful

My Tasks

Today I'm celebrating

date _____

Day 65

My Goal

#

My Affirmation for Today

My Schedule

Details

Notes

The Celebration Journal

Respect your own journey. If you missed the mark, can you celebrate coming close?

How positive did I stay today? ◯◯◯
How productive was I today? ◯◯◯

Daily Tracker

Relaxation

Meals

Today I'm grateful

My Tasks

Today I'm celebrating

www.shadowriverbooks.com

date _____

Day 66 | My Goal | #

My Affirmation for Today

My Schedule | Details

Notes

The Celebration Journal

The best-laid plans can fail, but the story isn't over.
The trick is to use what you've learned and move on.

How positive did I stay today?
How productive was I today?

Daily Tracker

Relaxation

Meals

Today I'm grateful

My Tasks

Today I'm celebrating

www.shadowriverbooks.com

date _____

Day 67 | My Goal | #

My Affirmation for Today

My Schedule

Details

Notes

The Celebration Journal

Trying doesn't guarantee success.
But guess what not trying guarantees.

How positive did I stay today?
How productive was I today?

Relaxation

Daily Tracker

Meals

Today I'm grateful

My Tasks

Today I'm celebrating

www.shadowriverbooks.com

date _____

Day 68   My Goal   #

My Affirmation for Today

My Schedule   Details

Notes

The Celebration Journal

Do you want to look back and wonder if you could have succeeded with a little more effort?

How positive did I stay today? ○○○
How productive was I today? ○○○

Relaxation

Daily Tracker

_____ ☐   _____ ☐
_____ ☐   _____ ☐
          ☐   _____ ☐

Meals

Today I'm grateful

My Tasks
- ○
- ○
- ○
- ○
- ○
- ○
- ○
- ○
- ○
- ○

Today I'm celebrating

www.shadowriverbooks.com

date _____

Day 69 | My Goal

#

My Affirmation for Today

My Schedule

Details

Notes

The Celebration Journal

No matter how an endeavor ended, it's usually possible to find something that came from it worth celebrating.

How positive did I stay today?

How productive was I today?

Daily Tracker

Relaxation

Meals

Today I'm grateful

My Tasks

Today I'm celebrating

www.shadowriverbooks.com

date _____

Day 70

My Goal

#

My Affirmation for Today

My Schedule

Details

Notes

The Celebration Journal

Be careful to ask for help in a way that respects the other person and yourself.

How positive did I stay today?

How productive was I today?

Daily Tracker

Relaxation

Meals

Today I'm grateful

My Tasks

Today I'm celebrating

www.shadowriverbooks.com

date _____

Day 71 | My Goal

\#

My Affirmation for Today

My Schedule

Details

Notes

The Celebration Journal

We tend to believe our Inner Critic,
but the truth is that voice is often a liar.

How positive did I stay today? ○ ○ ○
How productive was I today? ○ ○ ○

Daily Tracker

Relaxation

Meals

Today I'm grateful

My Tasks

Today I'm celebrating

www.shadowriverbooks.com

date _____

Day 72 | My Goal | #

My Affirmation for Today

My Schedule

Details

Notes

The Celebration Journal

Are you using deadlines and targets to beat yourself up? Can you find a better motivation?

How positive did I stay today?
How productive was I today?

Daily Tracker

Relaxation

Meals

Today I'm grateful

My Tasks

Today I'm celebrating

www.shadowriverbooks.com

date _____

Day 73

My Goal

#

My Affirmation for Today

My Schedule

Details

Notes

The Celebration Journal

Too often, failures loom large in memory while we forget what we've accomplished.

How positive did I stay today? ○○○
How productive was I today? ○○○

Relaxation

Daily Tracker

Meals

Today I'm grateful

My Tasks

Today I'm celebrating

www.shadowriverbooks.com

date _____

Day 74

My Goal

#

My Affirmation for Today

My Schedule

Details

Notes

The Celebration Journal

Be kind to yourself. It's good practice
for the way you want to live with others.

How positive did I stay today? ○○○
How productive was I today? ○○○

Daily Tracker

Relaxation

Meals

_____ ☐   _____ ☐
_____ ☐   _____ ☐
_____ ☐   _____ ☐

Today I'm grateful

My Tasks

○
○
○
○
○
○
○
○
○
○

Today I'm celebrating

www.shadowriverbooks.com

date _____

Day 75

Room for Improvement

My Schedule

Details

Notes

The Celebration Journal

If you're feeling blocked, look for something that is causing you to be confused or conflicted.

How positive did I stay today?
How productive was I today?

Daily Tracker

Today I'm grateful

Relaxation

Meals

My Tasks

Today I'm celebrating

www.shadowriverbooks.com

date _____

Day 76 My Goal

#

My Affirmation for Today

My Schedule

Details

Notes

The Celebration Journal

If you can't enjoy the journey, you may be on the wrong path.

How positive did I stay today? ○ ○ ○
How productive was I today? ○ ○ ○

Relaxation

Daily Tracker

_____ ☐   _____ ☐
_____ ☐   _____ ☐
_____ ☐   _____ ☐

Meals

Today I'm grateful

My Tasks
○
○
○
○
○
○
○
○
○
○

Today I'm celebrating

www.shadowriverbooks.com

date _____

Day 77 My Goal

\#

My Affirmation for Today

My Schedule

Details

Notes

The Celebration Journal

Being willing to change shows flexibility and humility.

How positive did I stay today? ○○○
How productive was I today? ○○○

Relaxation

Daily Tracker

_____ ☐   _____ ☐
_____ ☐   _____ ☐
_____ ☐   _____ ☐

Meals

Today I'm grateful

My Tasks
○
○
○
○
○
○
○
○
○

Today I'm celebrating

www.shadowriverbooks.com

date

Day 78 | My Goal | #

My Affirmation for Today

My Schedule

Details

Notes

The Celebration Journal

Dry spells may be signaling a need for a break. Refill the well with creative play.

How positive did I stay today? ☐☐☐
How productive was I today? ☐☐☐

Daily Tracker

_____ ☐   _____ ☐
_____ ☐   _____ ☐
_____ ☐   _____ ☐

Relaxation

Meals

Today I'm grateful

My Tasks

○
○
○
○
○
○
○
○
○
○

Today I'm celebrating

www.shadowriverbooks.com

date _____

Day 79

My Goal

#

My Affirmation for Today

My Schedule

Details

Notes

The Celebration Journal

Don't hold yourself to impossible standards. There will be days when survival is all you can hope for.

How positive did I stay today? ⬤⬤⬤
How productive was I today? ⬤⬤⬤

Daily Tracker

Relaxation

Meals

Today I'm grateful

My Tasks

Today I'm celebrating

www.shadowriverbooks.com

Day 80

date _____

My Goal

#

My Affirmation for Today

My Schedule

Details

Notes

The Celebration Journal

Don't let yesterday's failures encroach on today.
You're being given a brand new chance.

How positive did I stay today? ◯◯◯
How productive was I today? ◯◯◯

Daily Tracker

Relaxation

Meals

Today I'm grateful

My Tasks

Today I'm celebrating

www.shadowriverbooks.com

Day 81

date _____

My Goal

#

My Affirmation for Today

My Schedule

Details

Notes

The Celebration Journal

When progress is slow, can you celebrate trying something new or making a move that scared you?

How positive did I stay today? ○○○
How productive was I today? ○○○

Relaxation

Daily Tracker

Meals

Today I'm grateful

My Tasks

Today I'm celebrating

www.shadowriverbooks.com

date _____

Day 82

My Goal

#

My Affirmation for Today

My Schedule

Details

Notes

The Celebration Journal

We may not all be stars, but we can all still shine.

How positive did I stay today? ⬛⬛⬛
How productive was I today? ⬛⬛⬛

Daily Tracker

Relaxation

Meals

Today I'm grateful

My Tasks

Today I'm celebrating

www.shadowriverbooks.com

date

Day 83

My Goal

#

My Affirmation for Today

My Schedule

Details

Notes

The Celebration Journal

When you feel stymied, it helps to walk away. Literally. Take a walk. Take a shower. And wait.

How positive did I stay today?
How productive was I today?

Daily Tracker

Relaxation

Meals

Today I'm grateful

My Tasks

Today I'm celebrating

www.shadowriverbooks.com

date _____

Day 84 | My Goal | #

My Affirmation for Today

My Schedule | Details

Notes

The Celebration Journal

Facing one problem after another is discouraging so break the chain. Right now, it's just this one.

How positive did I stay today? ○○○
How productive was I today? ○○○

Relaxation

Daily Tracker

_____ ☐   _____ ☐
_____ ☐   _____ ☐
_____ ☐   _____ ☐

Meals

Today I'm grateful

My Tasks
☐
☐
☐
☐
☐
☐
☐
☐
☐
☐

Today I'm celebrating

www.shadowriverbooks.com

Day 85

date _____

My Goal

\#

My Affirmation for Today

My Schedule

Details

Notes

The Celebration Journal

Don't see people in your life as obstacles to your goal.
We are taught to love one another for a reason.

How positive did I stay today?

How productive was I today?

Daily Tracker

Relaxation

Meals

Today I'm grateful

My Tasks

Today I'm celebrating

www.shadowriverbooks.com

date _____

Day 86

My Goal

#

My Affirmation for Today

My Schedule

Details

Notes

The Celebration Journal

You can choose today whether to be
your own best friend or your own worst enemy.

How positive did I stay today?
How productive was I today?

Daily Tracker

Relaxation

Meals

Today I'm grateful

My Tasks

Today I'm celebrating

www.shadowriverbooks.com

date _____

Day 87   My Goal   #

My Affirmation for Today

My Schedule   Details

Notes

The Celebration Journal

Peak experiences may be followed by depression.
Sometimes we have trouble letting go of the struggle.

How positive did I stay today?

How productive was I today?

Daily Tracker

Relaxation

Meals

Today I'm grateful

My Tasks

Today I'm celebrating

www.shadowriverbooks.com

date _____

Day 88 | My Goal

#

My Affirmation for Today

My Schedule

Details

Notes

The Celebration Journal

Being busy is not the same as being productive.
Learn to love the open spaces in your schedule.

How positive did I stay today? ◯◯◯
How productive was I today? ◯◯◯

Relaxation

Daily Tracker

_____ ▢   _____ ▢

_____ ▢   _____ ▢

_____ ▢   _____ ▢

Meals

Today I'm grateful

My Tasks

◯
◯
◯
◯
◯
◯
◯
◯
◯

Today I'm celebrating

www.shadowriverbooks.com

date _____

Day 89 | My Goal | #

My Affirmation for Today

My Schedule

Details

Notes

The Celebration Journal

A contemplative life is often at odds with getting things done. Can you make room for both?

How positive did I stay today? ○○○
How productive was I today? ○○○

Daily Tracker

_____ ☐   _____ ☐
_____ ☐   _____ ☐
_____ ☐   _____ ☐

Today I'm grateful

Relaxation

Meals

My Tasks

Today I'm celebrating

www.shadowriverbooks.com

date _____

My Most Satisfying Victories

My Schedule

Details

Notes

The Celebration Journal

Resist the urge to keep tinkering.
Do your best, but when something is finished, let it go.

How positive did I stay today?
How productive was I today?

Daily Tracker

Relaxation

Meals

Today I'm grateful

My Tasks

Today I'm celebrating

www.shadowriverbooks.com

www.ingramcontent.com/pod-product-compliance
Lightning Source LLC
Chambersburg PA
CBHW030327100526
44592CB00010B/592